Tempo of Steam

CUMBRIAN COAST
EXPRESS

Nº 4498
CLASS   A4

Tempo of Steam

ROGER SIVITER

LONDON

IAN ALLAN LTD

First published 1980

ISBN 0 7110 1003 X

Published by Ian Allan Ltd, Shepperton, Surrey;
and printed by Ian Allan Printing Ltd at their works
at Coombelands in Runnymede, England

Dedicated to the memory of
Ken Blocksidge

Previous page: **A4 Pacific No 4498** *Sir Nigel Gresley* **at Steamtown
shed, Carnforth, on the morning of 11 July 1978, prior to working
light to Sellafield and returning with the 'Cumbrian Coast Express';
the outward train from Carnforth to Sellafield had been worked by
A3 Pacific No 4472** *Flying Scotsman*.

Below: **BR Standard Class 4 4-6-0 No 75027 climbs Freshfield Bank
on the Bluebell Railway with a Sheffield Park-Horsted Keynes train,
31 March 1975.**

Introduction

This book, which covers the period from 1966 to 1979, is my impression, through the lens of the camera, of some of the many different workings of the steam locomotive during that period.

For me it is a nostalgic journey, full of memories, of 'Britannias' and 'Black Fives' in the Lune Valley, A4 Pacifics in Scotland, NCB tank engines at Mountain Ash and Waterside, Porto Suburban, chime whistles in the Douro Valley, Port Elizabeth, Lootsberg Pass, the thrill of chasing a special — one could go on for ever because the list is endless. I hope to convey through this book the many happy hours I have spent on that nostalgic journey and would like to take this opportunity to thank all railwaymen whether they be professional or amateur for the help and co-operation shown to me.

The reader may be intrigued by the title of this book, *Tempo of Steam*, but as one of very many musicians interested in railways and the steam engine in particular the title is very appropriate. A steam engine in full cry has a tremendous rhythm about her, creating music in sight as well as sound.

No small part of the enjoyment for me is 'after the event' — by this I mean from the photographic point of view. I have spent many happy hours in the darkroom developing the negatives and then, such an important part developing the print. This is where I am able to create and compose from the basic material. The films I have used have been FP4, PANF and PLUS X, developed in D76, Acuspecial and latterly Aculux. All but the earliest pictures, which were taken with a Konica, were taken with Nikon cameras and lenses, my favourite lens being the 85mm.

In conclusion I would like to thank my wife Christina and Bob Williams for their help in the preparation of the book and Ann Slater for the typing.

ROGER SIVITER

Above: CP (Portuguese Railways) Henschel 4-6-0 No 292 near Tua in the Douro Valley with an evening train bound for Barca D'Alva on the Spanish border, 22 September 1974.

Below: Class 14CR 4-8-2 No 1897 shunts in the evening light of 25 July 1976 at Riversdale on the Worcester-George line in Cape Province (South Africa).

Top left: On the morning of 25 June 1966, 'Britannia' Pacific No 70009, formerly *Alfred the Great*, works light over Dillicar water troughs near Tebay, in the direction of Carlisle.

Left: No 70009 once again, this time on 13 September 1966 on the Settle-Carlisle line near Ais Gil summit with a southbound goods.

Above: 'Britannia' Pacific No 70014 *Iron Duke* on the Crewe-Carlisle line near Low Gill in the beautiful Lune valley, with a northbound goods on 31 August 1967.

Above: Narrow gauge 2-6-0T No E101, built by Esslingen, crossing Aroujo viaduct with a Lousade-Porto local train (northern Portugal).

Below: During the summer of 1973 A3 Pacific No 4472 *Flying Scotsman* worked on the 'Torbay Railway' in South Devon. No 4472 is pictured here on 22 July 1973 crossing Broadsands viaduct with a Paignton-Kingswear train.

Three photographs of Hunslet Austerity 0-6-0ST No 193 at work on the Severn Valley Railway.

Top left: Climbing between Eardington and Knowlesands with a Bridgnorth train, 31 December 1973.

Left: Leaving Bridgnorth with a Hampton Loade train, 31 December 1973.

Above: In woods south of Eardington with a Hampton Loade-Bridgnorth train, 1 April 1973.

13

Above: **Class 15AR 4-8-2 No 2083 leaving Port Elizabeth station (South Africa) with the 11.15 local train to Uitenhage on 29 July 1976.**

Top right: **Port Elizabeth again, this time a Class 15AR on Sydenham shed, 30 July 1976.**

Right: **South African narrow gauge in Cape Province: Class NG15 2-8-2 No 118 leaving Assegaaibos with the 09.15 to Avontuur on 28 July 1976.**

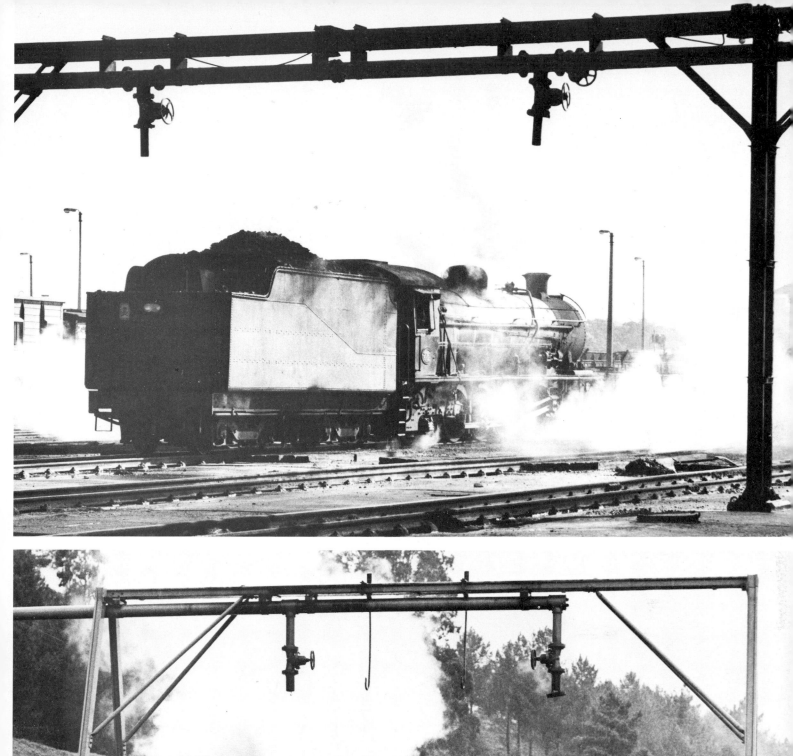

Above: On the afternoon of 26 September 1966, an Ivatt Class 2MT 2-6-0 No 46442 banks a goods train, bound for Stourbridge Junction, up the steep bank out of Halesowen towards Old Hill.

Right: Henschel 2-10-2 No 57017 blasts its way up a steep incline near Camlik, Western Turkey, with a Denizli-Izmir train on 22 February 1976.

Above: On 6 October 1978, No 7029 *Clun Castle* climbs through Camp Hill in the Birmingham suburbs, with a special train from Tyseley to Hereford, from where, on the following day, it worked another special to Chester and back.

Below: Class 9F 2-10-0 No 92220 *Evening Star* pulls out of York with the BR York circular train via Leeds and Harrogate, 9 July 1978.

Left: In the last months of BR steam Class 5 4-6-0 No 44887 pulls through Newton Heath (Manchester) with a northbound coal train on 18 November 1967.

Above: At Wirksworth Quarries, Derbyshire, on 23 February 1971, 0-4-0ST *Holwell No 3* built by Black Hawthorn in 1873, works empty hopper wagons from BR sidings.

Right: Class 5 4-6-0 No 44890 waiting to leave Preston station on 26 February 1968, with the 12.17 to Manchester Victoria.

Below: The DB Class 012 Pacifics worked out their last days on the Rheine-Emden line (West Germany). Pictured here on 21 March 1975 is No 012-055 near Meppen with an Emden-Rheine express.

Above: DB Class 023 2-6-2 No 023-040 waiting to leave Lauda Junction (southern Germany) with the 15.27 to Crailsheim, 25 March 1975.

Three scenes showing LNWR 'Precedent' class 2-4-0 No 790 *Hardwicke* on its return to steam during 1975-1976.

Above: At Steamtown shed, Carnforth, 1 May 1976.

Top right: North of Millom with trial run from Carnforth to Sellafield, in preparation for the Rail 150 celebrations, 22 July 1975.

Right: Being coaled at Steamtown prior to the above trial run, 22 July 1975.

Top left: On 14 June 1975 4-6-0s No 7808 *Cookham Manor* and No 6998 *Burton Agnes Hall* approach Colwall Tunnel, set in the Malvern Hills, with a Great Western Society special returning from Hereford to Didcot.

Above: Nos 7808 and 6998 once again — this time on 19 October 1974 climbing Hatton Bank with a GWS special from Didcot to Tyseley (via Stratford on Avon).

Left: On a beautiful September day in 1966 Class 5 4-6-0 No 45279 leaves Conway with a westbound goods.

Two views of Eskmeals viaduct south of Ravenglass with southbound special trains.

Top left: A3 No 4472 *Flying Scotsman* and B1 No 1306 *Mayflower* on 8 May 1976.

Centre left: A4 Pacific No 4498 *Sir Nigel Gresley* on 11 July 1978.

Bottom left: On 25 June 1978 V2 No 4771 *Green Arrow* is caught by the camera as it speeds through Bolton Percy with the BR York circular train.

Above: Former BR Class J27 0-6-0 No 2392, here with its original NER livery and class number (P3), storms out of Grosmont Tunnel with an afternoon train for Goathland (North Yorkshire Moors Railway) on 28 August 1972. This locomotive is now in the National Railway Museum, York.

Above: Portuguese Railways narrow gauge 0-4-4-0T No E169 waits in Povoa station for its next turn of duty, 30 May 1976.

Below: Portuguese Railways 2-8-2T No E143 storms out of Senora Da Hora with a local train for Porto Trindade on 2 June 1976.

Above: Henschel 4-6-0 No 286 (built in 1910) leaves Tua in the Douro valley (northern Portugal) with an evening train to Regua, 22 September 1974.

Below: Senora Da Hora again, this time a Henschel 0-4-4-0T leaves with a local train to Porto, 2 June 1976.

Above: **It is 1 June 1968 and 'Britannia' class Pacific No 70013** *Oliver Cromwell* **is about to depart from Manchester Victoria station with a northbound special.**

Right: Class 5 4-6-0 No 45206 shunts parcels vans at Manchester Victoria on 1 June 1968.

Above: Garratt Power — South African Railways Class GMA
4-8-2+2-8-4 No 4126 built by Beyer Peacock climbs towards
Grootsbrakrivier with the George-Mossel Bay train on 26 July 1976.

Top right: Another GMA Garratt, this time built by Henschel,
No 4067, glows in the evening sun as it approaches Krow Beck with a
Worcester-George train, July 1976.

Right: South African Railways Class 25NC 4-8-2 No 3425 leaves
Modder River, on the famous De Aar-Kimberley main line, with a
northbound goods, 4 August 1976.

Two panned shots of the BR York circular train near Bolton Percy south of York.
Above: Class 9F 2-10-0 No 92220 *Evening Star* on 26 August 1978.
Below: Class 5 4-6-0 No 5305 on 23 July 1978.

Above: Lubin shed in southern Poland with Class TY51 2-10-0
No TY51-126 on 31 August 1975.

Below: SNCF 141R 2-8-2 No 375 on Sarreguemines shed, eastern
France, 3 June 1971.

Top right: DB 2-10-0 No 052-759 being coaled at Lauda Junction,
southern Germany, 25 March 1975.

Below right: Chabowka, southern Poland: a UNRA 2-8-0 (left) and
Class TY2 2-10-0 pause between shunting duties, September 1975.

Top left: **New Romney station RHDR on 30 March 1975. No 10** *Doctor Syn* **runs light through the station passing No 3** *Southern Maid* **waiting to leave on a Hythe train.**

Left: **Narrow gauge 0-8-0 No PX48-1736 simmers on Krosniewice shed, southern Poland, at the end of the day's work, 4 September 1975.**

Above: **Class 5 4-6-0 No 45132 pulls out of Shrewsbury with the 12.25 train to Chester, 29 October 1966.**

Above: **Mountain Ash, south Wales, was one of the last strongholds of industrial steam. Here outside cylindered 0-6-0ST No 1 propels a train out of the colliery yard towards Aberaman, 2 January 1973.**

Right: Sir Thomas Royden, **a Barclay 0-4-0ST, shunts wagons at Stourport power station on 1 November 1969.**

Below: **Keighley & Worth Valley Railway 0-6-0ST** *Fred* **approaches Haworth with a train from Keighley on 28 May 1973.**

Above: Working hard on the Rheine-Emden line near Block Hemsen on 22 March 1975 is a DB Class 043 2-10-0, No 043-121, with a northbound goods.

Below: One of the South African Railways magnificent Class 15CA 4-8-2s, No 2847, near Reyton with a Witbank-Pretoria evening goods, 12 August 1976.

Left: Hunslet 0-6-0ST does some evening shunting work at Haig Colliery, Whitehaven on 30 August 1973.

Below left: Waterside in Ayrshire: Barclay 0-6-0T No 24 leaving Minnevey Colliery with a load of coal for Dunaskin Washery, 30 August 1973.

Right: Another Waterside scene — this time Barclay 0-4-0ST No 10 shunting at Dunaskin, 6 June 1975.

Below: Waterstop at Halesowen. Ex-GWR 0-6-0PT No 8718 pauses for refreshment during shunting duties on 12 March 1966.

Above: Contrast at Regua, northern Portugal: CP 4-6-0 No 282 shunts vans for a Porto train, 23 September 1974.

Right: Italian Railways Crosti type 2-8-0 No 241-028 climbing a grade near Valdaora on the beautiful Brunico-San Candido line in northern Italy, 19 August 1974.

Top: Class 9F 2-10-0 No 92017 north of Carlisle with a down goods on 31 March 1966.

Centre: GWR Class 2251 0-6-0 No 3205 at work on the Severn Valley between Eardington and Knowlesands with a Hampton Loade-Bridgnorth train on 23 June 1973.

Bottom: Ex-WD 2-10-0 No 600 *Gordon* climbing to Knowlesands with a Bridgnorth train on 14 April 1974.

Top right: Another scene on the Severn Valley Railway: GWR 0-6-0PT No 5764 leaves Knowlesands Tunnel and coasts down to Bridgnorth with a train from Bewdley, 10 August 1974.

Right: North Yorkshire Moors Railway. Ex-J27 class 0-6-0 No 2392 rolls down to Grosmont station to take out a Goathland train, 28 August 1972.

Above: A4 Pacific No 60009 *Union of South Africa* storms out of Dundee near Camperdown Junction with an Edinburgh-Aberdeen train, 14 April 1979.

Below: BR Standard Class 4 4-6-0 No 75027 climbs Freshfield Bank on the Bluebell Railway with a Sheffield Park-Horsted Keynes train, 31 March 1975.

Above: At De Aar shed on the morning of 3 August 1976 South African Railways Class 25NC 4-8-4 No 3430 and a converted condenser 4-8-4 No 3503 wait for their next turn of duty.

Below: Taking water outside Povoa shed, northern Portugal, on the evening of 24 September 1974 is No E142, one of four magnificent narrow gauge 2-8-2T engines built by Henschel in 1931 for service on the Porto-Povoa line.

Top left: **Cadley Hill Colliery near Burton-on-Trent. 0-6-0ST** *Cadley Hill No 1* **built by Hunslet, shunting near BR Exchange Sidings, 24 March 1972.**

Left: **Manvers Main Colliery, Wath. Austerity 0-6-0ST taking water on 2 April 1970.**

Above: **NCB 0-6-0ST No 6, built by Bagnall, banks a heavy train out of Eccles Colliery, Backworth, Northumberland, towards Barraden on 6 August 1975.**

Above: Silhouetted against the skyline on a tip near Dunaskin Colliery Waterside, Ayr, in south-west Scotland is Barclay 0-4-0ST No 19 on 30 August 1973.

Top right: LNWR 2-4-0 No 790 *Hardwicke* crosses Eskmeals viaduct during its trial run from Carnforth to Sellafield and return, 22 July 1975.

Right: A Robert Stephenson 2-8-2 of the Turkish Railways with an evening local train from Izmir to Ciyli, 25 February 1976.

Left: **Class V2 2-6-2 No 4771** *Green Arrow* climbing from Bramhope Tunnel to Weeton with the York circular train on 25 June 1978.

Above: **Class 5 4-6-0 No 45421 climbs Grayrigg Bank north of Oxenholme with a Carlisle-bound goods on 16 September 1966.**

Right: **Two BR Class 4MT 2-6-0s, Nos 76038 and 76047, storm up Talerddig Bank with a Shrewsbury-bound train on 27 August 1966.**

Above: Class 8F 2-8-0 No 48423 climbs towards Blackburn near Low Barn with coal empties from Preston on 18 April 1968.

Right: Narrow gauge 2-6-0T No E86 runs light into Porto Trindade station, northern Portugal, on 24 September 1974.

Top left: 'Jubilee' class 4-6-0 No 45593 *Kholapur*, now preserved at Tyseley, pulls out of Wakefield Kirkgate station with a Leeds-bound goods on 22 September 1966.

Left: Alas a beautiful station that is no longer with us, ex-GWR Snow Hill station in Birmingham. Class 5 4-6-0 No 44872 enters the station on 30 April 1966 with a special to the Festiniog Railway in north Wales.

Above: York shed 1 May 1966: from left to right, a Class 4MT 2-6-0, Class B1 4-6-0 No 61238 and Class V2 2-6-2 No 60824.

Above: Preserved DB Class 24 2-6-2 No 24-009 working a special train from Stuttgart to Hausach near Bittelbronn in southern Germany on 21 April 1974.

Below: Henschel 2-10-0 No 56541 of the Turkish Railways storms out of Izmir with a morning train to Denizli on 24 February 1976.

Above: On 21 July 1966 Class 02 0-4-4T No W33 *Bembridge* leaves Ryde Esplanade station, Isle of Wight, and crosses Ryde Pier for Pier station.

Below: Another Class 02 tank, No W24 *Calbourne*, pauses at Brading station with a Ryde-Shanklin train, 21 July 1966.

Above: Lymington Town station on the evening of 21 July 1966 as Class 2MT 2-6-2T No 41316 waits to leave with a train for Brockenhurst on the Waterloo-Bournemouth main line.

Below: 'Merchant Navy' class Pacific No 35022 *Holland America Line* speeds through Basing with a Waterloo-Bournemouth express on 8 April 1966.

Left: Easter 1978 saw the return of steam over the Settle-Carlisle line. On Easter Monday (27 March) Class V2 2-6-2 No 4771 *Green Arrow* storms up to Ais Gill summit with the 'Norfolkman' return working back to Leeds, having worked the train north to Carlisle the previous Saturday.

Above: Class 5 4-6-0 No 45187 threads the beautiful Lune valley and crosses Dillicar water troughs with a parcels train for Carlisle on 16 September 1966.

Above: Contumil shed, Porto, northern Portugal, on 31 May 1969 with Pacific No 559 on turntable surrounded by a variety of motive power including 4-6-0s, 2-8-0s and 2-6-4Ts. This was the first day of the first Ian Allan tour to Portugal.

Below: Lubin shed, southern Poland, on 31 August 1975, with P31 2-8-2s, TY51 2-10-0s and TY47 2-8-2s on shed.

Above: LNER 'Shire' class 4-4-0 No 246 *Morayshire* and a Caledonian 0-4-4T storm out of Laurieston near Falkirk with a special train to Darlington, via Edinburgh, for the Rail 150 celebrations on 3 August 1975.

Top right: Ex-Crosti 9F class 2-10-0 No 92020 climbs out of Albrighton with a Shrewsbury-Wolverhampton goods on 9 November 1966.

Right: Class J38 0-6-0 No 65914 drifts down to Thornton Junction in Fife with a coal train from the Cowdenbeath direction, 16 June 1966.

Top left: Climbing northbound through a snowstorm at Horton in Ribblesdale with the first steam special over the Settle-Carlisle line for many years, is Class V2 2-6-2 No 4771 *Green Arrow*, 25 March 1978.

Left: Shunting stock at Leeds Central station on 2 April 1966 is Stanier Class 4MT 2-6-4T No 42689.

Above: Another picture at Leeds Central on 2 April 1966, with another 2-6-4T, No 42073, shunting vans.

Above: **Portuguese Railways narrow gauge 2-6-0T No E86, built by Esslingen in 1886, has its smokebox cleaned out at Povoa on 24 September 1974.**

Right: BR Standard Class 4MT 4-6-0 No 75002 on Croes Newyd shed, Wrexham, 13 March 1967.

Above: Climbing out of Porto on the evening of 2 June 1976 is narrow gauge 0-4-4-0T No E165 with a local train for Lousado.

Top right: Cockburn's Wine Lodge at Tua in the Douro valley forms the background to a Tua-Mirandela train hauled by a narrow gauge 2-6-0T of Portuguese Railways, 22 September 1974.

Right: On a beautiful summer's day, Class 5 4-6-0 No 44899 rounds the curve at Low Gill in the Lune valley with a southbound goods, 31 August 1967.

Above: 'Castle' class 4-6-0 No 4079 *Pendennis Castle* near Church Stretton with a Shrewsbury-Newport special on 6 April 1974.

Top right: No 4079 again, this time climbing out of Hereford near Dinmore with a Newport-Shrewsbury special on 6 April 1974.

Centre right: GWR 4-6-0s No 7808 *Cookham Manor* and No 6998 *Burton Agnes Hall* climb out of Henley in Arden with a GW Society special from Didcot to Tyseley via Stratford-on-Avon on 19 October 1974.

Bottom right: Climbing up Hatton Bank bound for Tyseley is another GW Society special, this time hauled by No 6998 and No 5900 *Hinderton Hall*, 15 May 1976.

84

Below: Storming out of Rio Tinto with an evening Porto-Braga train is 2-6-4T No 096 on 2 June 1969. Note the handsome chain worn across the front buffer beam, a common practice at one time on Portuguese locomotives.

Above: Portuguese Railways 0-4-4-0T No E161 is busy shunting at Povoa on the evening of 24 September 1974.

Top left: Night time at Porto Trindade station. On 24 September 1972 2-8-2T No E141 fills up with water before taking out a local train.

Left: 'Crab' 2-6-0 No 42700 in store at Oxenhope shed on the Keighley & Worth Valley Railway, 22 April 1973.

Above: 'West Country' Pacific No 34015 *Exmouth* and 'Battle of Britain' Pacific No 34066 *Spitfire* seen at Salisbury shed on 7 April 1966.

Right: No 7029 *Clun Castle* speeds through Harbury cutting with a special train organised by the Birmingham *Sunday Mercury* newspaper on 16 April 1978, from Birmingham to the GW Society Open Day at Didcot.

Above: **No 4472** *Flying Scotsman* **storms out of Carnforth with the 'Cumbrian Coast Express' to Sellafield on 11 July 1978.**

Right: **'Hall' class 4-6-0 No 6998** *Burton Agnes Hall* **climbs into Worcester Shrub Hill station with a special train from Hereford bound for Didcot, 24 June 1973.**

Above: GWR 'Manor' class 4-6-0 No 7819 *Hinton Manor* **crosses the Victoria Bridge with a Bewdley-Arley train (Severn Valley Railway) on 29 December 1977.**

Below: **South African Railways Class 24 2-8-4 No 3970 on the picturesque branch from George to Knysna in Cape Province. The train is seen here crossing the Kaaimans River Bridge near Wilderness on 27 July 1976.**

Above: **No 6998** *Burton Agnes Hall* **crosses the Severn at Worcester with a special train for Hereford on 24 June 1973.**

Below: **Class V2 2-6-2 No 60813 approaches Perth with a morning train from Dundee, 21 June 1966.**

Above: Class A4 Pacific No 60019 *Bittern* leaves Perth with a morning Glasgow-Aberdeen express, 17 June 1966.

Below: No 4498 *Sir Nigel Gresley* storms up Lindal Bank near Dalton with the 'Cumbrian Coast Express' returning from Sellafield to Carnforth, 26 July 1978.

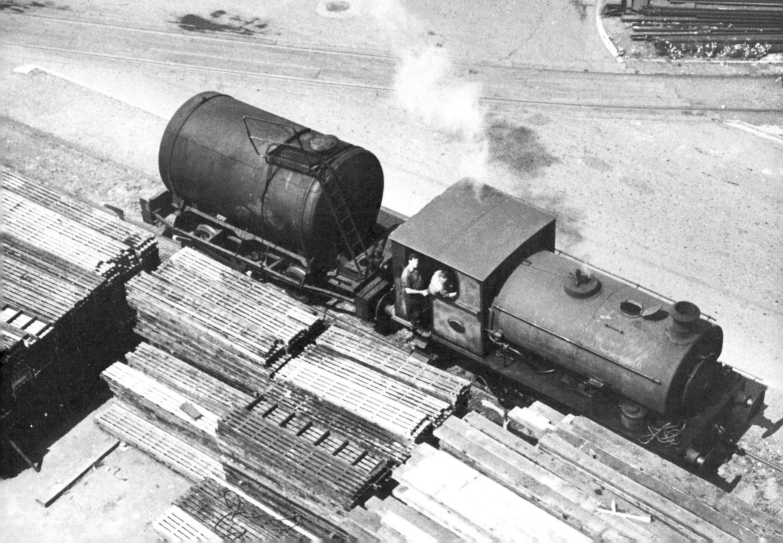

Top left: Rose Grove shed, Burnley, at the end of BR steam on 19 July 1968.

Left: Hudswell Clarke 0-4-0ST shunting petrol wagons at Falmouth Docks, 31 July 1968.

Above: On 2 January 1973, 0-6-0ST No 1 approaches Mountain Ash Colliery from Aberaman.

Above: **Former SR 4-6-0 No 841** *Greene King* **leaves Wanstead on the Nene Valley Railway with a Nene Park train on 27 May 1978.**

Below: BR Standard Class 5MT 4-6-0 No 73093 hurries over Aynho troughs south of Banbury with a York-Bournemouth train on 13 August 1966.

Above: 'Terrier' 0-6-0T No 323 *Bluebell* does some light shunting
duties at Horsted Keynes on the Bluebell Railway, 16 April 1977.

Below: 'Battle of Britain' Pacific No 34064 *Fighter Command* enters
Basingstoke with a down train on 7 April 1966.

Above: Standard Class 5 No 73133 and Class 5 4-6-0s on Patricroft shed, Manchester, 1 June 1968.

Right: Reflections at Lostock Hall shed, Preston — Class 8F 2-8-0 No 48253 on 25 February 1968.

Above: The Cromford and High Peak line on 20 May 1966; 0-6-0ST No 68066 near Newhaven with a train of empties for Middleton.

Below: Class 9F 2-10-0 No 92220 *Evening Star* near Horton in Ribblesdale on the 30 September with a special train from the West Riding of Yorkshire to Appleby for a memorial service for the late Bishop Eric Treacy.

Top left: **Former LNER Class A2 Pacific No 60530** *Sayajirao* **at Dundee shed on 17 June 1966.**

Left: **Class 5 4-6-0 No 44932 and A4 Pacific No 4498** *Sir Nigel Gresley* **at Steamtown shed, Carnforth, 11 July 1978.**

Above: **A South African Railways' 6th class 4-6-0 at Sydenham shed, Port Elizabeth, 30 July 1976.**

103

Left: Dundee 14 April 1979: A4 Pacific No 60009 *Union of South Africa* climbs out of Tay Bridge station with a special train for Aberdeen.

Above: Sir Nigel Gresley pauses at Dent station with a special to Carlisle, 21 October 1978.

Above: Evening at Povoa: narrow gauge 0-4-4-0T No E169 at rest outside the shed, 30 May 1976.

Below: Portuguese Railways compound 4-6-0 No 355 shunts in Barreiro shed yard near Lisbon, 7 June 1969.

Left: A Class 5 4-6-0 takes water at the south end of Preston station, 26 February 1968.

Above: An immaculate Class 15F 4-8-2 of the South African Railways receives attention at Newcastle shed on 11 August 1976. These engines worked in tandem on the Newcastle-Utrecht branch.

Below: Polish Railways Type P31 2-8-2 on Lubin shed, 31 August 1975.

Top left: A pair of DB Class 050 2-10-0s speed through Trossingen in southern Germany with a Rottweil train, 20 April 1974.

Left: South African Railways Class GMA Garratt No 4080 starts the long climb over the Lootsberg Pass with a Graaft Reinet-bound train on 1 August 1976.

Above: The evening sun glints on Portuguese Railways 4-6-0 No 291 on the turntable of Contumil shed, Porto, on 2 June 1969.

Top left: Class N2 0-6-2T No 4744 pulls out of Rothley for Loughborough on the Great Central Railway, 18 February 1979.

Left: Severn Valley Railway, 18 March 1979: GWR pannier tank No 5764 with a Bewdley-Bridgnorth train between Northwood and Arley.

Above: 'Jubilee' class 4-6-0 No 5690 *Leander* climbing out of Leeds near Horsforth with a special train to Carnforth, 24 February 1979.

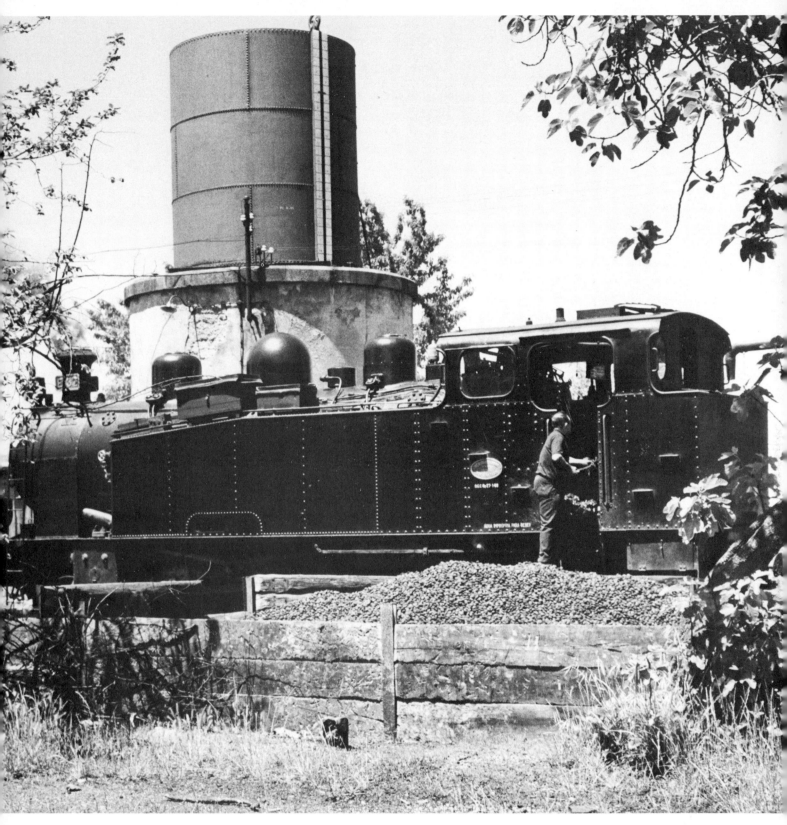

Left: GWR 0-6-0PT No 5764 at Bridgnorth station Severn Valley Railway, 30 June 1973.

Above: Portuguese Railways narrow gauge 2-8-2T No E132 being coaled at Visieau after working in with a train from Sernada Do Vouga on 5 June 1969.

Above: **The immaculate 'Royal Scot' 4-6-0 No 6115** *Scots Guardsman* makes a fine sight as it climbs out of Chinley with a train for York on 10 November 1978.

Right: **David Shepherd's engine, Class 9F 2-10-0 No 92203** *Black Prince*, storms out of Westbury with a special train for Eastleigh on 20 April 1975.

Waterloo scenes.

Top left: '**Merchant Navy**' **Pacific No 35012** *United States Line* **leaves with the 'Bournemouth Belle' on 29 May 1966.**

Left and above: '**Battle of Britain**' **Pacific No 34090 at rest after bringing in a Bournemouth train on 5 June 1967.**

Above: Former LMS Pacific No 6201 *Princess Elizabeth* near Church Stretton with the Inter-City special from Hereford to Shrewsbury on 24 April 1976.

Below: The unusual combination of LNWR 2-4-0 *Hardwicke* and A3 Pacific *Flying Scotsman* which are seen skirting the sea near Grange over Sands in Cumbria with a special to Sellafield, 8 May 1976.

Above: LNER Class K1 2-6-0 No 2005 arrives at the magnificent station at Stockton on Tees with a special from Middlesbrough to Newcastle, 22 October 1978.

Below: An Izmir-Denizli train south of Torbali Junction hauled by Turkish Railways 2-10-0 No 56541, 24 February 1976.

123

Left: On the day England won the World Cup, 30 July 1966, 'Jubilee' class 4-6-0 No 45565 passes through Salwick on the Blackpool-Preston line with an eastbound passenger train.

Above: Evening at Stoke shed — a Class 5 4-6-0 under the coaling tower on 24 April 1966.

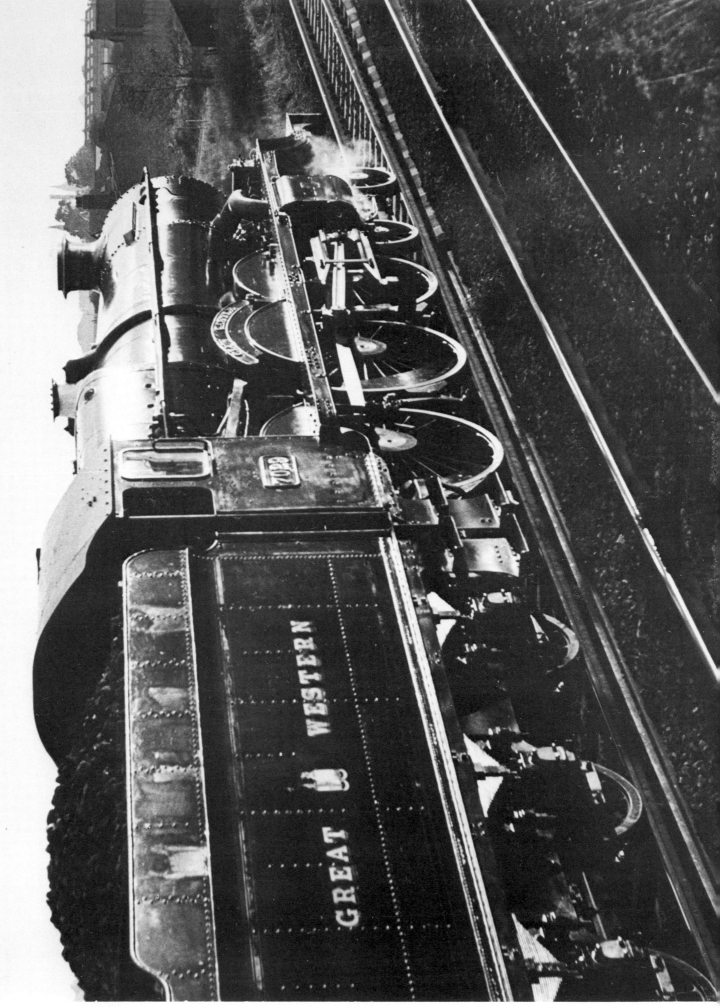

Above: BR Standard Class 4MT 4-6-0 No 75016 backs into Shrewsbury station to take out the down 'Cambrian Coast Express' on 25 October 1966.

Below: No 7029 *Clun Castle* glints in the evening sun as it climbs out of Birmingham through Camp Hill with a train for Hereford, 6 October 1978.

127

Above: Sunset at Kingswear. GWR 2-6-2T No 4588 poses on
Waterhead viaduct opposite Dartmouth, 23 July 1973.